A MAP PREDETER E

# A MAP PREDETERMINED AND CHANCE

LAURA WETHERINGTON

THE NATIONAL POETRY SERIES
SELECTED BY C. S. GISCOMBE

FENCE BOOKS

ALBANY · NEW YORK

Published in the United States by Fence Books, Science Library 320,
University at Albany, 1400 Washington Avenue, Albany, NY 12222,
www.fenceportal.org

Fence Books is a project of Fence Magazine, Incorporated, which is funded
in part by support from the New York State Council on the Arts and the
National Endowment for the Arts, along with the generous sponsorship of
the New York State Writers Institute and the University at Albany. Many
thanks to these friends and to all Friends of Fence.

Fence Books are distributed by Consortium Book Sales & Distribution
(cbsd.com) and printed in Canada by The Prolific Group (prolific.ca)

Design by Fence Books.
Cover art by Caitlin Murphy.

Library of Congress Cataloguing in Publication Data
Wetherington, Laura [1972– ]
A Map Predetermined and Chance/ Laura Wetherington

Library of Congress Control Number: 2011938341

ISBN 13: 978-1-934200-49-0

FIRST EDITION
10 9 8 7 6 5 4 3

# ACKNOWLEDGEMENTS

Grateful acknowledgment is made to the following journals, where these poems were first printed:

*21 Stars Review:* "This field is a blazon," "I'm right about time"

*Bombay Gin:* "That woman was found where all the dogs gone"

*Little Red Leaves:* "The open glass of water," "Long way from Cuyahoga Falls," "Weather patterns"

*Oxford Magazine:* "There is nothing funny about a penis"

*Starfish Poetry:* "Dancing the be-hop"

*Verse:* "In the day I dream in future tense: past sedative plus perfect," "Quiet people are crazy in bed"

# THE NATIONAL POETRY SERIES

was established in 1978 to ensure the publication of five poetry books annually through five participating publishers. Publication is funded by the Lannan Foundation; Stephen Graham; Joyce & Seward Johnson; Glenn & Renee Schaeffer; Juliet Lea Hillman Simonds; and Edward T. Cone Foundation.

## 2010 COMPETITION WINNERS

Lauren Berry of Houston, Texas, *The Lifting Dress*
Chosen by Terrance Hayes, published by Penguin Books

William Billiter of Clinton, New York, *Stutter*
Chosen by Hilda Raz, published by University of Georgia Press

James Grinwis of Florence, Massachusetts, *Exhibit of Forking Paths*
Chosen by Eleni Sikelianos, published by Coffee House Press

M.A. Vizsolyi of New York, New York, *The Lamp with Wings: Love Sonnets*
Chosen by Ilya Kaminsky, published by HarperCollins Publishers

Laura Wetherington of Roanoke, Virginia, *A Map Predetermined and Chance*
Chosen by C.S. Giscombe, published by Fence Books

III. VISITING NORMANDY

*for Jessica Milligan, Edie Gonzales, and Audrey Lauterbach*

## IN THE DAY I DREAM IN FUTURE TENSE: PAST SEDATIVE PLUS PERFECT

the present is a pasture:
a funny joke about pointers. it points to itself.
my vagina is a closed circuit television.
but how can one question with a period.

there is no narrator, no barrier.
I know how to see with my cells.
oscillate does not mean vacillate. both could mean masturbate:
my vagina is an electrical engineer.

THERE IS NOTHING FUNNY ABOUT A PENIS

## IF YOU MEET ME AND YOU FORGET ME THAT'S NOTHING BUT IF YOU MEET JESUS CHRIST AND YOU FORGET ABOUT HIM YOU ARE A BIG, FAT LOSER

We'll clean out the fireplace and put candles in it.
I'll try to tell you none of this is who we are.
Of course I won't lose you
because I never had you to begin with.

What is the verb to have?
I have internal organs: borrowed from the moment.
Okay, sorry, it's not about this moment.
It's about a fleet of moments.

Or we'll clean out the fireplace
and burn trees in it.
I'll try to tell myself of course I won't lose
what I borrowed from the earth.

What is the verb to have to?
I have internalized a distant fleeting somewhere off.
Wow. None of this is who we are.

It's not about this fireplace.
Somewhere, it's about death.
Because I never had none of this.

I can't see you when you're here
because it's death I love.

## QUIET PEOPLE ARE CRAZY IN BED

All orgasm is just me clapping for myself on the inside.
We are sound waves reverberating in the chambers of our skin.
We are sound whales crooning the universe in.

# I LOVE YOU LARGELY

If my va gina were gi ant

I'd let you
**MOVE IN.**

## You slip through my fingers

This is a verb: your fingers.
This is a noun: my
desire. They make
a sentence: you finger
my desire.

This is a sentence:
the verb I have for you is not a-spectual;
I will spread your glottis —
form my mouth around your clitic.
This sentence does not rhyme.
                    What does it do?
It reads like a primer; my primer
is a desire: see my desire get
fingered. You hold it in
your hands: this paper.
Wait.

We can switch theta roles
(you are the patient;
I want you here in the words
where I am the dictor.)
I want to explore your deep
structure.
              Map it out on paper.
           This paper.
Wait.
This is a sentence.
And this is a sentence.

# I MEASURE THE FOREST BY MY TREE

I can't keep time with Mozart.
        I will violate your hymen.
Drama regards the virgin as a mother.
                I'm a generation of out to get me.


There is no going back from this kind of selfishness.
        Violins call out what I will do to you.
I muscle in on your moon phase.
                My tongue makes you mute.


I'm almost in puberty with respect to this situation.
        Light disappears behind your head.
All valleys are unarmored.
                I'm not straight on this.


Figure yourself in slow motion.
        Your vagina is a country.
Your orgasm takes over agriculture.
                Memory becomes a tribute to stealing.

## STROKING THE BIRD'S TAIL

this is why there is no color in the evening
a wind unhinged undressed a body turning over in a bed wheeling sweat and from the weather
her memory is not there but in a hassock bolted on both sides folded over she is a burro and a mouth attached to
a face an open mouth
bites her she bruises the arch of a foot then a leg
wakes up she's missing a leg still from the unrest was she resting

this is why we still see her in the photo someone put their finger on the trigger pulled it
no longer her arm lifting tai chi meeting ceiling
no evening then her arm flickers in the wind winding unnerving toward her velvet path
ringing the doorbell running away and yesterday the porch the banister butter yellow the front door bright red
the heat unfolding painting daytime there purpled in the bed
she opens the door then one foot enclosed in a slipper leading to this joint in her hip and the bend in her wrist
the same movement

and the breathing the weather is breathing her breeding wishing the negative tai chi arm blocking
this is why red maple leaves are purpled they are heat
rising to the surface and they are escaping she calls out your sleep name

# To Travis or Dennis or Sam

You were just a
**JAZZ-**
**HOLE**

I

*passed*

*through*

on my way to the
**BLUES**.

## ALL I WANT IS UNIVERSE

It has to do with trees.

We are sleeping past and
presents.

Why are you water? What am
I holding? What am I water?

Little bean, what does it
mean?

I am longing      I am no
thing          not a bad thing

You are the hum that makes me
undone. You are everyone.

# II.
# An Ordinary
# So Necessary

# My poitrine made of clouds

*after Yves di Manno*

For so long I have looked
for a memory expansive
as my own.

Today I write; I wait for
the form around which
I was formed.

I was formed inaugural.
I was formed a picture.
You cannot abolish
my eyes and my sense.

## LONG WAY FROM CUYAHOGA FALLS

I am almosting it.

Go then.

what wha where are [you] what.

Crude 60 you 60

rail rail

Man.

Come on.

Pig Wish for Lowe High School

rail rail rail rail

Ah, Dwntn

No.

no no no [no] Let me.

4 Luv 4 ooooh.

arrow up

arrow down

GO GOODY

What was. This this.

# WEATHER PATTERNS

*after Paul Claudel*

i.
Explain to me the river: water choosing its continent. Between the
entirety of one land mass and a prism that unravels light I march in.


ii.
I am a river long and unknotted, descending like tornadoes, without
remorse, the same ocean of elbows for rivers and not longer.


iii.
I wasn't long. I fall regularly like rainfall or more than I can, which is
to say that I take a long time to fall into gold light.


iv.
This decoration of light is softness without cease and in necessary
order. I am one part combatant, one part immigrant one part
coincidence.


v.
International passages make light of my fits and starts. An idea is
essential to lose.

# Dancing the be-hop

LXXV.

Woman of the principle use: beehive she bop mishap
the syllables go la
la da dee
go long. They go laaaaa

Women of the principal. [she goes on clapping. she's clap-happy.]
And the clock woman, she goes on the prince of limping.
That next day was a clap-a-day
the fat-tastic dee go long, go laaaaa

And when the principal dancers came in,
they made long lines of CONCESSION STANDS
and lined up their young rows with mumps. Plump ones.
The big to-do list went long      it went laaaaa
and danced through

XIX.

I went dominating the shes, I went sidelining the shocks, I went eating
     the ages of ears.
It's a jumpalong, Cassidy. (it's a beehop).
The next thing about the v: to propose impropriety:
a vivisection :: an erectomy.
(don't tell your mother it's venerating,
not relevant to the present situation, i.e.
there are chains of prepositions: over, under, in.)

Your mom's a climb.
Something I've sewn up. Yr mom's a little something.
So on a vacation. So plump. So impossible. So what.
And now, brought to you by the ocean: whispered: dismay.

Paper to its end, agro bodies. Acrobats. Any possible somewhere. Any
     possible long. And plus and plus and plus. We ain't so number
     one.

III.

When I blow open the sidelong and scream out LOUT and LOUDER I
am speaking events that happened to me, shoving them into the shed
in the back. Out falls a shovel and the dog makes a dig at the slippers.
What I meant to say about the mind HAPPENED TO ME and the space of
mental breakdown is that this happens to WHY ARE YOU DOING THIS TO
ME all of us on some level though we may repress it for Jungian reasons
of letting someone else live out our memories.

XI.

Oh, the pope. He go hmmmm and the song starts. She was already
singing it in his head. The pope looks different because he's a changed
man. He goes hmmmmm. He thinks it's all about.

I'm pushing a projection line and lining up a profession. A
processional of young white robes in yellow teeth and naked
underneath. This man leaning out of the left cathedral window going
Laaaaaa, he go laaaaaaaaaa.

Not the valve of betrayal. (Jesus) Not because the eyelid flutters (or
doesn't) she is blind. Color folded in the ANATOMY of the people. The
people's anatomy game starting to buck they system. Unequivocated
laaaaaa. And I asked for a lawyer.

Her masectomy. Later, to cut the bonsai into a standing woman in
armor, flexing her check-paw. Barely compression, the night in. I want
to lay out a bit of hope for your coming under the door like a letter.
First, fold one leg over the other. Then put your forehead to the floor.
Sure, it's dirty. Sure, I'm waiting. I'll wait.

XXII.

If this continues on the contingency of nakedness,
I'm afraid I'll have to undress.
At least undo. I'm closing my hymen (come close, come close)
I'm closing my human. STAMP ON IT.

Put things in a picture and bind it in leather to see the seams
[someone else's ass on the line.] Shit ain't supposed to be funny; it's
supposed to be crazy. Heir man, what hand did god have in making
all of this possible to be missed? Are you missing it? What would it
take to be convinced of something you don't already know? [a regular
envelope.]

# THE ENCOUNTERED

*after Roland Dubillard*

It seems
we were born without rights
until we are given a name—my name
is legal and I ask myself

As long as my right hand is connected to me
my name is made like clouds.
My encountered will follow, the birds
will follow I will develop into
trouble, my name is legal
who would retain me?

The wingspan lengthens.
All around me are fields
and the clouds cross my non-sight.

And me a believer of names.
My belief is legal—it is a
sharp color. These colors touch
me and I open. My right place
calms, my right eye and birds
are legal.

# THIS FIELD IS A BLAZON

*for Tara Grant*

There's a boundary around her body;
yellow lye holds her in the earth in wintertime.

*That arm is mine,* she sings.
It's as though she's floating.

*I'm serious,* he swore, and buried her leg. He buried her severed head.
This will show the world what it is to cross the line.

*I'm not kidding,* he said, and smoked the shovel
into her back. When she went down,

he helped her all the way.
This is what it means to love.

*I'm not joking,* she said, and headed for the door.
Through her teeth she swore, *Never again.* He agreed.

# I'M RIGHT ABOUT TIME

*Who can use words untruthfully enough*
*To build eternity inside his own short mouth.*
                                    —*Laura Riding*


Time was immemorial
and in between a time


time was mean all the while
mean and while and time was


we was children.
Time was we was virgins.


Time was fast forward.
Children fly out of the mouths of children.


Young girls grow bark which we have to peel away.
Children fly out of my mouth and peel away.


I wish I had a magic carpet and children.
We all flew from mouths.


You swore you was from the womb of a woman.
Mouths flew out of my mouth and peeled away.

Time was a timid body. I say timid.
Time was less fruit and fruitful in between.


Time wasted. I was an apple in the end.
How long does it take time to age? It's ageless.


And what would be your favorite time
and want would be and immemorial.


Time was and time wasn't.
Time wasn't. That's what it was.


Meanwhile, time I memorized.
The breathing was tight. Time opened up the night in my diaphragm.

# HE SAID THE FULLNESS OF THE UNIVERSE IS A FLEETING FEELING

The connection of hunching over and a table in a bar
silences his eyes falling through his eyes—
both arms spread around a scream like wings,
momentary gaps of things falling, waves thudding,
sounds of breathing housed in a metaphor that lives in water.
His house is made of time.

# THE LIFE WORTH LIVING IS MADE

When I was born, I woke up
in the crook of the living. The young
morning yawned its mourning.
I awoke to the thighs of the dead.

When I woke up, I was under
the weather. Where I was born,
I bore into the arms of the living,
whether or not they were dead.

Once, I was born through the legs of the living.
My elected love,
tell me your name.

                 Once I was born,
the dead loved living. Whether or not I was loved,
or living, whether or not I was legs,

the life worth living is dead.
Mother, whisper your name.
Whether or not I am sleeping, love,
sing me your dead.

# No one wants to play the victim no one when there is a gun involved and blue

the victim wears blue stockings the victim is dead perpetrated your
sister rides the bus in blue stockings the victim is a tuesday vicious
vicious vicious vixen no one fucks with the victim no one rings on
the phone drops a line gives a shout-out says hello no one is the
victim's friend the victim's enemy is no one wears things like joy and
exuberance took a left turn the victim there on the bus and the side
of the bus has a hotline number for enemies of victimhood which
means the victim is second to no one and no one is dead winning
a story means an apex and someone has to get the punch so what is
there about blame and conflict that the victim complains about it's a
livelihood i'm telling you death is lively and it's a luckihood and the
enemy of the victim wears blue stockings like a hood a face-warmer a
head-mitten and the victim fights back and sometimes climaxes that
means winning

the beautiful part of living is getting to choose who you are the victim
chooses victimhood the victim is only playing learns the meaning of
continent and incontinence in the same sentence the victim's wrists
are wrinkled the victim makes fists throws fits the victim is into fisting
the victim is into deep shit and now it turns into the want the victim
doesn't want

no one will print up flyers for the disappearance of the victim and
plaster them to brick buildings and lamp posts no one's slogan no one's
headline no one's candlelight vigil no one has registered the victim's
dog with the licensing bureau not the neighbor not the postman not

the bus driver and not the victim no one killed the dog no one buried it the dog is not the dog of the victim and the victim is not the dog of the victim sam is not the victim frank sally susan no victim not victim the victim is not missing the point or a dog that is dead the victim is free like an ion the dog is the shortstop the catcher the apprentice to dying the victim can be a drag getting up in the morning the morning being the middle of the night and the victim seeing whose face face the mirror the non-entity no one you are not fat you are not fat you are not and the gun and the dog and the climax and the victim lives in a little house with no back door

# Nature a map predetermined and chance

We cannot get away from the way our minds solidify:

wood becomes lightning which turns back into wood

while the lightning peels past gravity

far far past the human eye against lines of force this is our eyelight.

Movement is a cliff always falling when we are at sea.

The wave comes through our feet, the duende,

then shoots out eyelightning like thunder we are quiet.

We choose into what we cannot get out of:

the way we hold our bodies.

We hold a boat of lightning in our hands.

Therefore, we are light into wood in the sea,

which is a shorthand for misunderstanding

or a shorthand for anything out of reach.

In whichever way we meander backwards from falling

everyone is hello and everyone a wave

then a sea change.

# THE OPEN GLASS OF WATER

I'm owning up the ocean
god and you impossible
god impress you  impossible
your vestibule an investment in its own barrier
liver of the reflection in vestments iridescent

unpleasantness dresses itself as a threat
I'm owing up to your illevel
an ordinary so necessary

oh, illevel     oh, polutress

I'm owning your investments polutress

less investment iridescent to its own barrier

unpleasantness as ordinary as the ocean

and oh reflection as a threat

reflection of a window in a window

oh, illevel     oh, dress of threat

# THAT WOMAN WAS FOUND WHERE ALL THE DOGS GONE

Them dogs are long since laid under and he keep asking, *Why do
women exist why do women exist why do women exist.*

Feeling blue, he keep thinking,
How dark the water.

The lampshade lay
next to the open window. It was summer.

The lampshade a thrown grenade that exploded the bulb.
He thumbed her down and she bubbled up blue.

Her mouth gasped for air her mouth gaping
her hair a mat of blue.

He undered her—pumped her chest like an emergency rescue
until she was only the space in the middle of her brain.

Each rib, a wing.
*Fly away, you.*

# MICHAEL ONDAATJE AS BILLY THE KID
## DESCRIBES MADNESS

Michael Ondaatje as Billy the Kid
describes madness as a man who in-bred dogs
until they mutated into depravity and ate him alive.

In the story, all the townspeople were surprised
by the end to the man who was crazy
but did not appear crazy
when he came into the bar, several times a week,
to drink with the soldiers.

But secretly he bred dogs.
Or, not secretly, because
his mom gave him the money to buy the dogs,
and everyone knew this was his project.

But no one knew he was crazy. Or,
they might've known a little bit, because
he tried to kill his mom once, and if you
try to shoot someone, you are crazy.
(Except if you're a soldier
and you go to the bar a lot.)

The thing is, no one knew *how* crazy he was.
He hadn't tried to kill his mom since, so maybe
the townspeople thought he'd gotten over it
(and building a high fence in your backyard
so no one can see in and then breeding dogs there
for years without ever selling them or
letting anyone see them doesn't make a person crazy.)

He didn't want to show those
dogs to anyone till he had gotten them right,
he said. And of course no one blinked at that.
For some artists, when they are working on a new creation,
there's a period where they don't show their work.
To anyone. And the impulse to want to create,
that's not madness. It's beautiful.

# III.
# Visiting Normandy

Johnson gave a great speech,
saying Victory, Liberation, Death to the enemy,
Some of the men would have to die,
Peace cost a price, and so on. Then he said,
*I want to shake the hand of each one of you tonight, so line up.*
And he reached down, pulled his knife from his boot
and raised it high above his head,
promising in a battle cry:
*Before dawn of another day,*
*I'll sink this knife*
*into the heart of the foulest bastard in Nazi land.*
A yell burst from all 2,000 of the men.

The first four days after
arriving I'm staying in
a dorm room for high-
schoolers who commute
from far-away farms. The
room has a steel frame
bed and a desk. A naked
bulb hangs from the
ceiling. When I go out I
have to repeat my poor
French multiple times, so
mostly I stay in, keep the
blinds drawn, sleep into
the afternoon, and smoke
menthols.

He said the 501$^{st}$ code name was Klondike,
and their secret base was at Hamstead Marshall—
Lady Craven's estate—
about halfway between Newbury and Kintbury.

In Arabelle's class I'm trying to get the students to name French-speaking countries so I ask them, I say, *What accent does Céline Dion have?*

Four of the kids start laughing hysterically, falling out of their seats, hollering laughing because one of them has said she has an accent circumflex.

Then they boarded the aircraft.
It was still dusky daylight at Welford Air Field
as they took off in the first serial of forty-five C–47 airplanes.

Six hundred fifty paratroopers to lead the invasion of Europe.
He was in plane number 44
on the fifth row.

There would be twenty serials,
fifteen miles apart.
The Welford serial would land on drop zone C.

There were twenty-three paratroopers on plane 44.
He was seated
number twenty-three in the stick.

The flight time
from Portlandville to Utah Beach
would be fifty-seven minutes.

Fifty-four miles out they turned southeast,
flew over the Channel Islands, then turned due east
for the twenty-three miles over land.

Arabelle tells me in 1940 her grandfather
was taken to Germany as a prisoner,

before there were camps, so her grandfather
and her grandfather's best friend worked on a farm until

they managed to escape.
They traversed France and made it to Spain where

they were caught. Again they decided to escape.
After the first or second day they took up a tile

and dug a hole and that's where they put their instruments.
They filed their way through the bars

and somehow broke out through the sewage or drainage system.
This was after eight months.

When they got to the Straights of Gibraltar where the English
were, the English thought they were German spies.

They were imprisoned again for eight days.
They had swallowed their dog tags

and left a string hooked on their back molars
so they could pull them out again. Finally they were believed.

They made their way to England, became commandos
in the Free French Forces, and trained in Scotland.

Then the red light snapped on at the door.
*Stand up and hook up.*
There was the stamping of feet,
snap fasteners clicking shut on the static line.

They shuffled lockstep and halted,
ready to go. No one had to tell them
what it was when they heard it for the first time.
It sounded like rocks in a tin can.

Their plane began taking evasive action.
They continued to be hit.
The rock sounds came and went,
but they stayed up.

The green light popped on—
*Go Geronimo!* and they all jumped.
He'd never been so glad
to get out of a plane in his life.

The parachute slammed open;
the planes were gone, taking the tracers with them.

A friend who works for the arts bureau is letting me usher, in exchange for tickets. Arabelle and I go to *Voyage d'Hiver*.

The stage is black. There's a raised rotating platform with an iron bed frame on it, propped at a 45 degree angle.

One woman has super-short hair and two boots: one with a heel and a military one. Fishnet stockings. Sleeveless duster jacket. A leotard. All black.

Then there's the contra-tenor—he has the body of a farmer from the Midwest—and he wears a black skirt, a black leather vest, and no shirt.

The contra-tenor sounds like he's from a boy's choir and sings in German. The leotard lady reads Müller in French. Ilka, the red-headed mastermind of the troupe, wears a lot of different masks. She's nearly naked most of the time. They all have whitish makeup on.

In the last scene, Ilka has on a baby's-head mask (her face is exposed and has blood on it, and the mask part is an exaggeratedly large papier-mâché forehead and cranium,) and she has on a black skirt which makes that part of her blend into the stage, and she has baby legs coming out of her hips, crossed at the ankles, and a sled, too, made out of wood, and she's topless and covered in blood and she has two ski poles and she keeps turning her waist (the sled) like she's skiing.

So let me revise:
Ilka in a baby's head
with a woman's bare chest
and covered in blood
is skiing in a sled through the darkness.

And then all the lights turn off and that's it.

He said there was water everywhere below,
except just a small strip that he could see,
and he was drifting
dangerously close to the water.

He pushed his thumbs into the saddle
of the chute, sat down, and quickly unbuckled his leg straps,
preparing for water landing.
He was working on his chest straps

when his shoe caught a small tree
and he smashed into the marsh.

So Arabelle and I are laughing
about how embarrassing
it would be to have to go
to the pharmacy and ask
for something for a yeast
infection, except not knowing
the word for yeast infection,
I'd have to describe: *It's in
the legs, here, in the woman's
place, and it itches* and the
pharmacy man would ask,
*Can you repeat that?* because I
wouldn't be describing it well
and I'd keep doing the hand
motion for itching down by
my legs and meanwhile more
and more people would be
getting in line behind me.

All the drugstore things are in a special pharmacy store
and I have to ask the pharmacist for them—even Tylenol.
I have to say, I want Tylenol for my headache
and then the guy explains
how many to take and when.

He got out of his chute
with his knife and moved forward
to John Fordik, then to Swift,
who was struggling to walk.
Bravo joined them along the way;
they helped Smith forward
until they reached the number thirteen man
at the river's edge
as it turned inward
into a wide expanse of water.
There was no sound from the water.
It was obvious then that the first twelve men of plane 44 had drowned.

Arabelle says there's a laboratory in the U.S.
where they take your ashes
after you've been cremated
and compress them into a diamond.

He found the company medic
who had been caught by the Germans
as he came down.
He was hanging in a tree by his feet,
his arms down,
throat cut,
genitals stuffed in his mouth.
His medic's red-cross armband
was stained with the blood
that had flowed from his hair.

Arabelle's mom died when she was five and a half.
For two years her dad told her
that momma was sick and in the hospital
and one day she and her friend were arguing at recess over marbles
and she said to her friend,
she said, *I'm going to tell my mom when she comes back*
and her friend hollered,
*Your mom's not coming back she's been dead for two years!*

Arabelle stopped speaking.
The principal laid into Arabelle's father
and her grandfather, the commando,
from the Free French Forces, he laid into him, too,
he said to the dad,
*You see what you've done?*
*I told you to tell her*
*but you didn't and now she's traumatized*
*with a wound that may never close and why?*
*Marbles?*

I run into Arabelle's class
outside the movie theater—
I'm at the laundromat.

I look up
and Carry and Illias are waving at me.
So I run outside and yell *Hello!*
and wave my arm like my life depends on it
and they keep waving
and they holler back, *Hello! Hello! Hello!*

It completely makes my day.

When daylight came,
they stopped on a hillside
along a dirt road,
set out their land mines in a giant circle,
and pulled out their D-ration chocolate bars
and canteens and ate breakfast.
Meyer, Bravo, Fordik and he
sat down together and talked it over,
deciding which way to go.

For Valentine's Day
my mom sends stickers for all the kids,
so I use the English phrase that the kids know,
and say to them, *I love my mother*
and then in French, *Do you know why?*
Sofian says, *Because she's beautiful?*
and Cyril says, *Because she's sick?*

# NOTES

VISITING NORMANDY
    The accounts of D-Day are from an oral history transcript of Lt. Carl H. Cartledge. University of New Orleans Eisenhower Center. June 14, 1988.

LONG WAY FROM CUYAHOGA FALLS
    The line "I am almosting it" comes from James Joyce's *Ulysses*.


# A THOUSAND THANK YOUS

So many people have been instrumental in helping me form my thoughts and words, I won't be able to list them all. Still, I want to make a small gesture of thanks to those folks who shaped my understanding of poems and the world of the mind: Stan Rushworth, Okua Omosupe, Joseph Stroud, Trent Tano, Charles Altieri, Sue Schweik, Zack Rogow, Geoffrey G. O'Brien, John Shoptaw, The Lunch Poems Reading Series, Ray Lifchez, Nimrod (mille mercis!), Helen Zell, Raymond McDaniel, Khaled Mattawa, Linda Gregerson, Marie Howe, Lorna Goodison, Thylias Moss, Laura Kasischke, T Hetzel, Katie Hartsock, Josh Edwards, Lauren Proux, Sam Mock, Chris Pruitt, Karyna McGlynn, Michelle Chan Brown, KC Trommer, Anya Cobler, David Ruderman, Randa Jarrar, Taiyaba Husain, Delia DeCourcy, Anna Vitale, Adam Fagin, the New England Literature Program staff and students, the Hopwood Room, Andrea Beauchamp, Nicholas DelBanco, Stephanie Stio and the National Poetry Series, and all the folks at *Fence*. A special shout out to Jeremy Buchmann. Of course I owe *everything* to my family. I particularly want to thank my brother, Cole, who, in the fourth grade, taught me how writing can be funny by drawing on my face in black magic marker while I was sleeping... I'm coming for you, bro.

# *FENCE*
## *BOOKS*

Fence Books has a mission to redefine the terms of accessibility by publishing challenging writing distinguished by idiosyncrasy and intelligence rather than by allegiance with camps, schools, or cliques. It is part of our press's mission to support writers who might otherwise have difficulty being recognized because their work doesn't answer to either the mainstream or to recognizable modes of experimentation.

The Motherwell Prize is an annual series that offers publication of a first or second book of poems by a woman, as well as a five thousand dollar cash prize.

The Fence Modern Poets Series is open to poets of any gender and at any stage of career, and offers a one thousand dollar cash prize in addition to book publication.

For more information about either prize, or more informatin about *Fence*, visit www.fenceportal.org.

## National Poetry Series

| | |
|---|---|
| A Map Predetermined and Chance | Laura Wetherington |
| The Network | Jena Osman |
| The Black Automaton | Douglas Kearney |
| Collapsible Poetics Theater | Rodrigo Toscano |

## The Motherwell Prize

| | |
|---|---|
| Negro League Baseball | Harmony Holiday |
| living must bury | Josie Sigler |
| Aim Straight at the Fountain and Press Vaporize | Elizabeth Marie Young |
| Unspoiled Air | Kaisa Ullsvik Miller |

## The Alberta Prize

| | |
|---|---|
| The Cow | Ariana Reines |
| Practice, Restraint | Laura Sims |
| A Magic Book | Sasha Steensen |
| Sky Girl | Rosemary Griggs |
| The Real Moon of Poetry and Other Poems | Tina Brown Celona |
| Zirconia | Chelsey Minnis |

## Fence Modern Poets Series

| | |
|---|---|
| The Other Poems | Paul Legault |
| Nick Demske | Nick Demske |
| Duties of an English Foreign Secretary | Macgregor Card |
| Star in the Eye | James Shea |
| Structure of the Embryonic Rat Brain | Christopher Janke |
| The Stupefying Flashbulbs | Daniel Brenner |
| Povel | Geraldine Kim |
| The Opening Question | Prageeta Sharma |
| Apprehend | Elizabeth Robinson |
| The Red Bird | Joyelle McSweeney |

## Anthologies & Critical Works

*Not for Mothers Only: Contemporary Poets on Child-Getting & Child-Rearing*
Catherine Wagner & Rebecca Wolff, editors

*A Best of Fence: The First Nine Years, Volumes 1 & 2*
Rebecca Wolff and Fence Editors, editors

## Poetry

| | |
|---|---|
| *Mercury* | Ariana Reines |
| *Coeur de Lion* | Ariana Reines |
| *June* | Daniel Brenner |
| *English Fragments / A Brief History of the Soul* | Martin Corless-Smith |
| *The Sore Throat & Other Poems* | Aaron Kunin |
| *Dead Ahead* | Ben Doller |
| *My New Job* | Catherine Wagner |
| *Stranger* | Laura Sims |
| *The Method* | Sasha Steensen |
| *The Orphan & Its Relations* | Elizabeth Robinson |
| *Site Acquisition* | Brian Young |
| *Rogue Hemlocks* | Carl Martin |
| *19 Names for Our Band* | Jibade-Khalil Huffman |
| *Infamous Landscapes* | Prageeta Sharma |
| *Bad Bad* | Chelsey Minnis |
| *Snip Snip!* | Tina Brown Celona |
| *Yes, Master* | Michael Earl Craig |
| *Swallows* | Martin Corless-Smith |
| *Folding Ruler Star* | Aaron Kunin |
| *The Commandrine & Other Poems* | Joyelle McSweeney |
| *Macular Hole* | Catherine Wagner |
| *Nota* | Martin Corless-Smith |
| *Father of Noise* | Anthony McCann |
| *Can You Relax in My House* | Michael Earl Craig |
| *Miss America* | Catherine Wagner |

## Fiction

| | |
|---|---|
| *Prayer and Parable: Stories* | Paul Maliszewski |
| *Flet: A Novel* | Joyelle McSweeney |
| *The Mandarin* | Aaron Kunin |

F
B